An Interactive Journal for Kids

201 THINGS TO PRAY ABOUT

SHILOH kidz
An Imprint of Barbour Publishing, Inc.

Written and compiled by Jessie Fioritto.

Print ISBN (Boys) 978-1-64352-317-0

Print ISBN (Girls) 978-1-64352-318-7

Published by Shiloh Kidz, an imprint of Barbour Publishing, Inc., 1810 Barbour Drive, Uhrichsville, Ohio 44683, www.shilohkidz.com

Our mission is to inspire the world with the life-changing message of the Bible.

ecpa Member of the Evangelical Christian Publishers Association

Printed in China.

000090 0220 HA

YOU CAN TALK TO GOD ABOUT ANYTHING!

"Call to Me, and I will answer you."

JEREMIAH 33:3

You can talk to God! About anything and everything. The One who created you cares about every part of your life—from the big things to the smallest detail. This whole giant universe is under His care, and He wants to hear from *you*. Your prayers can change things—they might even change your life! All you have to do is ask, and the powerful God of everything promises to listen to all your concerns and answer you. Isn't that amazing? He's available 24-7, anytime you need Him. Are you ready to begin the adventure of deeper prayer with God? This journal will ensure you don't run out of things to talk about. So what are you waiting for? Turn the page and discover 201 topics to jump-start your chats with God.

"Then you will call upon Me
and come and pray to Me,
and I will listen to you."
JEREMIAH 29:12

1. YOUR FAMILY

Do you think God really hears every word you pray?

2. YOUR FRIENDSHIP WITH JESUS

"I do not call you servants that I own anymore. A servant does not know what his owner is doing. I call you friends, because I have told you everything I have heard from My Father."

JOHN 15:15

3. YOUR FRIENDS

How does your friendship with Jesus change the way you live?

4. YOUR NEIGHBORS

"For God so loved the world that He gave His only Son. Whoever puts his trust in God's Son will not be lost but will have life that lasts forever."

JOHN 3:16

5. YOUR SCHOOL

Does prayer really change anything?

6. YOUR TEACHERS

Bring up a child by teaching him the way he should go,
and when he is old he will not turn away from it.
PROVERBS 22:6

7. YOUR FUTURE

What kinds of things do you pray about most?

8. WISDOM IN CHOOSING YOUR FRIENDS

Iron is made sharp with iron,
and one man is made sharp by a friend.

PROVERBS 27:17

9. YOUR PLANS

When you pray, do you usually ask for what you want or what God wants?

10. THAT YOU RECOGNIZE WHEN YOU ARE BEING TEMPTED

"Watch and pray so that you will not be tempted. Man's spirit is willing, but the body does not have the power to do it."

MATTHEW 26:41

11. YOUR VICTORIES

Has God ever answered your prayers in unexpected ways?

12. YOUR FAILURES

Then they cried out to the Lord in their trouble.
And He saved them.

PSALM 107:19

13. YOUR STRUGGLES

Can you talk to God about anything?

14. YOUR STRENGTHS

God has given each of you a gift. Use it to help each other. This will show God's loving-favor.

1 PETER 4:10

15. YOUR FEARS

Has God ever answered your prayer by saying no?

16. YOUR SAFETY

The Lord is my light and the One Who saves me. Whom should I fear? The Lord is the strength of my life. Of whom should I be afraid?

PSALM 27:1

17. PRAISE GOD THAT HE IS ALWAYS IN CONTROL!

Does God always have your best in mind?

18. YOUR COUNTRY

When those who are right with God rule, the people are glad,
but when a sinful man rules, the people have sorrow.

PROVERBS 29:2

19. YOUR MISTAKES

Does God still love us even when we mess up?

20. THE THINGS YOU WANT

"First of all, look for the holy nation of God. Be right with Him. All these other things will be given to you also."

MATTHEW 6:33

21. THE THINGS YOU NEED

Can God really take care of all our needs?

22. GOD'S FORGIVENESS

If we tell Him our sins, He is faithful and we can depend on Him to forgive us of our sins. He will make our lives clean from all sin.

1 JOHN 1:9

23. YOUR ATTITUDE

Do you pray to God throughout the day?

24. THAT YOU WOULD NOT COMPLAIN OR WHINE

A glad heart is good medicine,
but a broken spirit dries up the bones.

PROVERBS 17:22

25. YOUR HAPPINESS

Do you think God ever makes mistakes?

26. CONTROLLING YOUR ANGER

A gentle answer turns away anger,
but a sharp word causes anger.
PROVERBS 15:1

27. YOUR SADNESS

Does God really want to be our friend?

28. YOUR ENEMIES

*"But I tell you, love those who hate you. (*Respect and give thanks for those who say bad things to you. Do good to those who hate you.) Pray for those who do bad things to you and who make it hard for you. Then you may be the sons of your Father Who is in heaven."*

MATTHEW 5:44–45

29. THAT YOU CAN FORGIVE THOSE WHO HURT YOU

Should you pray for people who are mean?

30. YOUR WORDS

So comfort each other and make each other strong as you are already doing.

1 THESSALONIANS 5:11

31. YOUR SIBLINGS

Is there anything God can't do?

32. YOUR COUSINS

Agree with Him in all your ways,
and He will make your paths straight.
PROVERBS 3:6

33. YOUR CHURCH

Does God actually care about our problems?

34. YOUR PASTOR

As He saw many people, He had loving-pity on them. They were troubled and were walking around everywhere. They were like sheep without a shepherd. Then He said to His followers, "There is much grain ready to gather. But the workmen are few. Pray then to the Lord Who is the Owner of the grain fields that He will send workmen to gather His grain."

MATTHEW 9:36–38

35. YOUR YOUTH MINISTER

Should we pray every day?

36. THAT YOU WOULD BE KIND TO THE UNKIND

God has chosen you. You are holy and loved by Him. Because of this, your new life should be full of loving-pity. You should be kind to others and have no pride. Be gentle and be willing to wait for others.

COLOSSIANS 3:12

37. YOUR PEACE

If God knows everything, why do we need to pray?

38. THANK GOD THAT HE NEVER CHANGES!

Jesus Christ is the same yesterday and today and forever.

HEBREWS 13:8

39. YOUR DOCTOR

Do you need to use fancy words when you pray?

40. ENDANGERED SPECIES

Then God said, "Let Us make man like Us and let him be head over the fish of the sea, and over the birds of the air, and over the cattle, and over all the earth, and over every thing that moves on the ground."

GENESIS 1:26

41. THAT YOU WOULD TRUST GOD

Do you believe God always answers prayer?

42. SOMEONE WHO HAS MADE FUN OF YOU

Put out of your life all these things: bad feelings about other people, anger, temper, loud talk, bad talk which hurts other people, and bad feelings which hurt other people. You must be kind to each other. Think of the other person.

EPHESIANS 4:31–32

43. THAT YOU WOULD HAVE A JOYFUL HEART

Do we have to close our eyes to pray?

44. PRAISE GOD THAT HE HAS A PLAN FOR YOUR LIFE!

"For I know the plans I have for you," says the Lord,
"plans for well-being and not for trouble,
to give you a future and a hope."

JEREMIAH 29:11

45. WISDOM TO KNOW WHAT IS TRUTH

Is everything in the Bible true?

46. YOUR RELIABILITY

Happy are those whose way is without blame,
who walk in the Law of the Lord.

PSALM 119:1

47. PERSECUTED CHRISTIANS LIVING AROUND THE WORLD

Why do some people pray to idols?

48. YOUR RESPECT FOR YOUR MOM AND DAD

"Honor your father and your mother, so your life may be long in the land the Lord your God gives you."

EXODUS 20:12

49. MISSIONARIES

Why do missionaries need a lot of prayer?

50. THAT YOU WOULD BE A LEADER AMONG YOUR FRIENDS

Do not let anyone fool you. Bad people can make those who want to live good become bad.

1 CORINTHIANS 15:33

51. CHILDREN WHO LIVE IN ORPHANAGES AROUND THE WORLD

What is prayer?

52. THE PRESIDENT OF THE UNITED STATES AND HIS FAMILY

A nation falls where there is no wise leading, but it is safe where there are many wise men who know what to do.

PROVERBS 11:14

53. YOUR FAITHFULNESS

Why is it good to pray?

54. PRAISE GOD THAT HE KNOWS EVERYTHING!

Have you not known? Have you not heard? The God Who lives forever is the Lord, the One Who made the ends of the earth. He will not become weak or tired. His understanding is too great for us to begin to know.

ISAIAH 40:28

55. THOSE WHO ARE SUFFERING

How does God feel when we pray?

56. YOUR COURAGE

"Have I not told you? Be strong and have strength of heart! Do not be afraid or lose faith. For the Lord your God is with you anywhere you go."

JOSHUA 1:9

57. THANK JESUS FOR HUMOR!

Does God have a sense of humor?

58. YOUR ATTITUDE TOWARD CHORES

Be glad you can do the things you should be doing.
Do all things without arguing and talking about
how you wish you did not have to do them.

PHILIPPIANS 2:14

59. YOUR BOLDNESS FOR JESUS

How can God be everywhere?

60. THANK GOD FOR HIS MERCY!

Let us go with complete trust to the throne of God. We will receive His loving-kindness and have His loving-favor to help us whenever we need it.

HEBREWS 4:16

61. YOUR COACHES

Can you talk to God about anything?

62. YOUR SCHOOL JANITOR

*"Let the greatest among you be as the least.
Let the leader be as the one who cares for others."*

LUKE 22:26

63. YOUR SCHOOL CAFETERIA WORKERS

Does how we pray matter?

64. THOSE WHO SERVE IN THE MILITARY

Fight the good fight of faith. Take hold of the life that lasts forever. You were chosen to receive it.

1 TIMOTHY 6:12

65. THAT YOU WOULD ALWAYS DO YOUR BEST

Can we pray anywhere?

66. CHRISTIANS LIVING IN THE MIDDLE EAST

"Let your light shine in front of men. Then they will see the good things you do and will honor your Father Who is in heaven."

MATTHEW 5:16

67. YOUR FRIENDS WHO DON'T KNOW JESUS

Why should you pray?

68. YOUR GENTLENESS

They must not speak bad of anyone, and they must not argue. They should be gentle and kind to all people.

TITUS 3:2

69. YOUR WORK ETHIC

Can we ask God to help us pass a test?

70. PRAISE GOD THAT HE HAS SAVED YOU THROUGH JESUS!

Because of the blood of Christ, we are bought and made free from the punishment of sin. And because of His blood, our sins are forgiven. His loving-favor to us is so rich.

EPHESIANS 1:7

71. THAT YOU WOULD SPREAD HOPE IN THE WORLD

Why should we go to God for help?

72. YOUR GRANDMA

But the fruit that comes from having the Holy Spirit in our lives is: love, joy, peace, not giving up, being kind, being good, having faith, being gentle, and being the boss over our own desires. The Law is not against these things.

GALATIANS 5:22–23

73. PERSECUTED CHRISTIANS LIVING IN NORTH KOREA

Why do we pray for our enemies?

74. PRAISE GOD BECAUSE HE IS AWESOME!

"For the Lord your God is the God of gods and the Lord of lords. He is the great and powerful God and is to be honored with fear. He does not show favor, and cannot be bought with money."

DEUTERONOMY 10:17

75. YOUR SCHOOL ADMINISTRATORS

Is it okay to pray a memorized prayer every time we pray?

76. YOUR HEART FOR SERVING OTHERS

Christian brother, you were chosen to be free. Be careful that you do not please your old selves by sinning because you are free. Live this free life by loving and helping others.

GALATIANS 5:13

77. THAT YOU WOULD STICK WITH JESUS NO MATTER WHAT

Why do we ask Jesus into our heart?

78. THAT YOU WOULD BE A GOOD FRIEND TO OTHERS

A friend loves at all times.
A brother is born to share troubles.
PROVERBS 17:17

79. YOUR FITNESS

Why do some people pray every night before bed?

80. YOUR WORRIES

Worry in the heart of a man weighs it down,
but a good word makes it glad.
PROVERBS 12:25

81. YOUR CHURCH MUSICIANS

Can we pray at any time?

82. PERSECUTED CHRISTIANS LIVING IN AFRICA

My Christian brothers, you should be happy when you have all kinds of tests. You know these prove your faith. It helps you not to give up. Learn well how to wait so you will be strong and complete and in need of nothing.

JAMES 1:2–4

83. YOUR YOUTH GROUP

What happens if you don't pray ever?

84. YOUR LOVE FOR OTHERS

*Those who do not love do not know
God because God is love.*

1 JOHN 4:8

85. PRAISE GOD THAT HE IS GOOD!

Does praying all the time make someone a better person?

86. YOUR MAIL CARRIER

Nothing should be done because of pride or thinking about yourself. Think of other people as more important than yourself. Do not always be thinking about your own plans only. Be happy to know what other people are doing.

PHILIPPIANS 2:3–4

87. YOUR LOCAL POLICE OFFICERS

Does God know everything?

88. STRENGTH TO DO THE RIGHT THING

Be sure your love is true love. Hate what is sinful. Hold on to whatever is good.
ROMANS 12:9

89. SOMEONE WHO MAKES YOU JEALOUS

If we do something wrong, can we still pray?

90. PRAISE GOD FOR THE BIBLE!

"Call to Me, and I will answer you. And I will show you great and wonderful things which you do not know."

JEREMIAH 33:3

91. UNSAVED MEMBERS OF YOUR FAMILY

What is a prayer warrior?

92. YOUR GOODNESS TO OTHERS

*We are His work. He has made us to belong
to Christ Jesus so we can work for Him.
He planned that we should do this.*

EPHESIANS 2:10

93. YOUR SCHOOL LIBRARIAN

How does God answer our prayers?

94. YOUR DAILY QUIET TIME WITH GOD

Put on the things God gives you to fight with.
Then you will not fall into the traps of the devil.
EPHESIANS 6:11

95. PERSECUTED CHRISTIANS LIVING IN PAKISTAN

Do we still have to pray even if we're tired?

96. THAT YOU WOULD BE A GOOD EXAMPLE TO OTHERS

Let no one show little respect for you because you are young. Show other Christians how to live by your life. They should be able to follow you in the way you talk and in what you do. Show them how to live in faith and in love and in holy living.

1 TIMOTHY 4:12

97. POLITICIANS IN YOUR GOVERNMENT

How does God hear millions of people praying all at once?

98. YOUR CONTENTMENT

I am not saying I need anything. I have learned to be happy with whatever I have.

PHILIPPIANS 4:11

99. YOUR GRANDPA

Does God only give us things that we need?

100. YOUR PATIENCE WITH OTHERS

Live and work without pride. Be gentle and kind. Do not be hard on others. Let love keep you from doing that.

EPHESIANS 4:2

101. PRAISE GOD THAT HE WILL NEVER LEAVE YOU!

Can anything separate you from God's love?

102. THAT YOU LOVE GOD WITH EVERY PART OF YOURSELF

"'You must love the Lord your God with all your heart and with all your soul and with all your mind and with all your strength.' This is the first Law."

MARK 12:30

103. YOUR CLASSMATES WHO ARE SAD

Why doesn't God give us everything we pray for?

104. THOSE WHO ARE HARD TO LOVE

Forgive other people just as God forgave you
because of Christ's death on the cross.

EPHESIANS 4:32

105. PEOPLE LIVING IN MEXICO

How can we “pray continually”?

106. THAT GOD WOULD GUIDE YOUR CHOICES

Trust in the Lord with all your heart, and do not trust in your own understanding. Agree with Him in all your ways, and He will make your paths straight.

PROVERBS 3:5–6

107. THE SPIRITUAL HEALTH OF YOUR FAMILY

Why doesn't God always answer prayers right away?

108. TELLING OTHERS ABOUT JESUS

Do not love the world or anything in the world.
If anyone loves the world, the Father's love is not in him.

1 JOHN 2:15

109. THAT YOU WOULD ALWAYS PUT GOD FIRST

Do we have to fold our hands to pray?

110. YOUR LOCAL FIREMEN

"No one can have greater love than to give his life for his friends."

JOHN 15:13

111. THAT YOU WOULD BE HUMBLE IN EVERY SITUATION

Why do we end prayers with "amen"?

112. THE HOMELESS IN YOUR COMMUNITY

God is our safe place and our strength.
He is always our help when we are in trouble.
PSALM 46:1

113. YOUR ATTITUDE ABOUT SCHOOL

Are there things that we shouldn't pray about?

114. THAT KIDS IN YOUR COMMUNITY WOULD SEE THEIR NEED FOR JESUS

He said to them, "You are to go to all the world and preach the Good News to every person."

MARK 16:15

115. THAT YOU WOULD LEAN ON JESUS WHEN YOU FEEL WEAK

Is it okay to complain to God when we're praying?

116. YOUR COMPASSION

Help each other in troubles and problems.
This is the kind of law Christ asks us to obey.
GALATIANS 6:2

117. YOUR SCHOOL SECRETARY

Does God care about our feelings?

118. THAT YOU WOULD KEEP YOUR MIND FIXED ON JESUS

Let us keep looking to Jesus. Our faith comes from Him and He is the One Who makes it perfect. He did not give up when He had to suffer shame and die on a cross. He knew of the joy that would be His later. Now He is sitting at the right side of God.

HEBREWS 12:2

119. CHRISTIANS LIVING IN INDIA

Will God listen to your prayers even though you're young?

120. PRAISE GOD FOR THE PEACE HE GIVES YOU!

"I have told you these things so you may have peace in Me. In the world you will have much trouble. But take hope! I have power over the world!"

JOHN 16:33

121. THAT YOU WOULD SHOW LOVE AND RESPECT TOWARD EVERYONE

Does God really control everything?

122. KIDS WHO ARE IN FOSTER CARE

"Learn to do good. Look for what is right and fair.
Speak strong words to those who make it hard for people.
Stand up for the rights of those who have no parents."

ISAIAH 1:17

123. YOUR AUNT

How do we pray?

124. THAT YOU WOULD TAKE CARE OF YOUR BODY

Do you not know that your body is a house of God where the Holy Spirit lives? God gave you His Holy Spirit. Now you belong to God. You do not belong to yourselves.

1 CORINTHIANS 6:19

125. YOUR UNCLE

Why did Jesus pray?

126. YOUR STATE SENATOR

*"You should choose from the people able men who fear God,
men of truth who hate to get things by doing wrong.
Have these men rule over the people, as leaders."*

EXODUS 18:21

127. PRAISE GOD FOR HIS FAITHFULNESS!

Can we pray for animals?

128. THAT YOU WOULD RESIST PEER PRESSURE

He who walks with wise men will be wise, but the one who walks with fools will be destroyed.

PROVERBS 13:20

129. THAT YOU WOULD OBEY YOUR PARENTS EVEN WHEN YOU DON'T FEEL LIKE IT

Should you pray for your friends?

130. THAT YOU WOULD LET GO OF GRUDGES

"Do not hurt someone who has hurt you. Do not keep on hating the sons of your people, but love your neighbor as yourself. I am the Lord."

LEVITICUS 19:18

131. YOUR SCHOOL PRINCIPAL

Can we pray about money?

132. YOUR RELATIONSHIP WITH GOD

What does the Lord ask of you but to do what is fair and to love kindness, and to walk without pride with your God?

MICAH 6:8

133. THAT YOU WOULD PUT OTHERS FIRST

Will God help us with our attitudes?

134. PRAISE GOD FOR ALL THE WAYS HE HAS HELPED YOU!

Give all your cares to the Lord and He will give you strength. He will never let those who are right with Him be shaken.

PSALM 55:22

135. PERSECUTED CHRISTIANS LIVING IN AFGHANISTAN

Will God help us choose our friends?

136. KIDS BEING TREATED IN CHILDREN'S HOSPITALS

Sing for joy, O heavens! Be glad, O earth! Break out into songs of joy, O mountains! For the Lord has comforted His people. He will have loving-pity on His suffering people.

ISAIAH 49:13

137. THAT YOU HONOR YOUR GRANDPARENTS

Can God help you with school?

138. THAT YOU WOULD KEEP YOUR LIFE PURE

Keep your heart pure for out of it are the important things of life.

PROVERBS 4:23

139. YOUR GARBAGE TRUCK DRIVER

Is it okay to be angry when you're praying?

140. YOUR MOM

Do not turn away from your mother's teaching.
For they are a glory to your head and a
chain of beauty around your neck.

PROVERBS 1:8–9

141. CHRISTIANS IN CHINA

Will God help you win at sports?

142. YOUR DAD

Hear your father's teaching, my son.

PROVERBS 1:8

143. PRAISE GOD THAT HE IS CREATIVE!

Why did God create you?

144. YOUR ATTITUDE ABOUT HOMEWORK

You have now become a new person and are always learning more about Christ. You are being made more like Christ. He is the One Who made you.

COLOSSIANS 3:10

145. THAT YOU WOULD USE SOCIAL MEDIA AND TECHNOLOGY IN A GOD-PLEASING WAY

How do our prayers show what's going on in our heart?

146. THAT GOD WOULD STRENGTHEN YOU TO ALWAYS BE HONEST

Do not lie to each other. You have put out of your life your old ways.

COLOSSIANS 3:9

147. YOUR VIDEO GAMES

Should you pray about being sad?

148. PEOPLE LIVING IN SOMALIA

"Those who have it very hard for doing right are happy, because the holy nation of heaven is theirs."

MATTHEW 5:10

149. THE JUDGES IN YOUR COUNTRY

How do you feel when God doesn't answer a prayer right away?

150. THAT YOU WOULD FIND FRIENDS WHO LOVE JESUS TOO

A man who has friends must be a friend, but there is a friend who stays nearer than a brother.

Proverbs 18:24

151. YOUR EATING HABITS

Should we pray only when we need something?

152. HIGH SCHOOL STUDENTS IN YOUR COMMUNITY

"Whoever calls on the name of the Lord will be saved from the punishment of sin."

ACTS 2:21

153. YOUR CHURCH WORSHIP LEADER

Does God get tired of answering prayers?

154. YOUR LOCAL PARAMEDICS

Save those who are being taken away to death.

PROVERBS 24:11

155. PRAISE GOD THAT HE LOVES YOU!

If we do something wrong, will God still love us?

156. FORGIVENESS FOR ANY TIME YOU HAVE BEEN UNKIND

For His loving-kindness for those who fear Him is as great as the heavens are high above the earth. He has taken our sins from us as far as the east is from the west.

PSALM 103:11–12

157. THE LIFEGUARDS IN YOUR COMMUNITY

Can you pray for God to send you a godly friend?

158. THAT YOU WOULD NOT BRAG

Let another man praise you, and not your own mouth.
Let a stranger, and not your own lips.
PROVERBS 27:2

159. THE CASHIER WHERE YOU SHOP

Can God help you find something you lost?

160. PRAISE GOD THAT HE MADE YOU UNIQUE!

I will give thanks to You, for the greatness of the way I was made brings fear. Your works are great and my soul knows it very well.

PSALM 139:14

161. THE ENVIRONMENT

Does God want us to take care of the planet?

162. THAT YOU WOULD BE KIND TO SOMEONE WHO NEEDS A FRIEND

"Do for other people what you would like to have them do for you."

LUKE 6:31

163. THAT YOU GET ALONG WITH YOUR SIBLINGS

What is the Lord's Prayer?

164. THANK GOD FOR ALL OF HIS GOOD GIFTS TO YOU!

Whatever is good and perfect comes to us from God. He is the One Who made all light. He does not change. No shadow is made by His turning.

JAMES 1:17

165. YOUR BUS DRIVER

Does God know what you're thinking?

166. FOR STRENGTH TO APOLOGIZE WHEN YOU HURT OTHERS

"If you take your gift to the altar and remember your brother has something against you, leave your gift on the altar. Go and make right what is wrong between you and him. Then come back and give your gift."

MATTHEW 5:23–24

167. YOUR JOY

Can God help you pray?

168. PRAISE GOD FOR HIS KINDNESS!

The Lord is full of loving-pity and kindness. He is slow to anger and has much loving-kindness.

PSALM 103:8

169. YOUR COMMUNITY LEADERS

Is it okay to ask God for something we don't really need?

170. THAT YOU WOULD RESPECT YOUR TEACHERS

Show respect to all men.

1 PETER 2:17

171. PRAISE GOD FOR THIS DAY THAT HE MADE!

Does God want us to be happy all the time?

172. GOD'S PROTECTION

But the Lord is faithful. He will give you strength and keep you safe from the devil.

2 THESSALONIANS 3:3

173. A FRIEND OR RELATIVE WHO IS SICK

Why doesn't God heal everyone who is sick?

174. YOUR FAVORITE TEACHER

"I have teaching and wisdom.
I have understanding and power."

PROVERBS 8:14

175. YOUR LEAST FAVORITE TEACHER

Do we have to pray to be forgiven?

176. YOUR FRIENDS WITH DIVORCED PARENTS

He heals those who have a broken heart.
He heals their sorrows.

PSALM 147:3

177. YOUR OBEDIENCE TO YOUR PARENTS

Why should we pray for missionaries in other countries?

178. YOUR HIGH SCHOOL ROLE MODEL

In all things show them how to live by your life and by right teaching. You should be wise in what you say. Then the one who is against you will be ashamed and will not be able to say anything bad about you.

TITUS 2:7–8

179. YOUR YOUTH GROUP LEADERS

Can we ask God for stuff that we want, like toys or a new bike?

180. THAT GOD WOULD TEACH YOU AS YOU READ YOUR BIBLE

"The Helper is the Holy Spirit. The Father will send Him in My place. He will teach you everything and help you remember everything I have told you."

JOHN 14:26

181. THAT YOU RESIST THE TEMPTATION TO TALK BACK TO YOUR PARENTS

What should we do when it seems like God isn't answering our prayers?

182. THAT YOU WOULD USE KIND WORDS

Pleasing words are like honey. They are sweet to the soul and healing to the bones.

PROVERBS 16:24

183. YOUR TEAMMATES

Will God hear our prayers if we don't talk out loud?

184. YOUR LOVE FOR GOD

"You will look for Me and find Me,
when you look for Me with all your heart."
JEREMIAH 29:13

185. THAT JESUS FOLLOWERS WOULD BE ELECTED AS LEADERS

Why do we have to thank God at every meal?

186. THAT YOUR FAMILY WOULD FOLLOW JESUS TOGETHER

Give me your heart, my son.
Let your eyes find joy in my ways.
PROVERBS 23:26

187. THE VICE PRESIDENT OF THE UNITED STATES AND HIS FAMILY

What things does God want us to pray about?

188. INMATES IN PRISON

The Lord is not slow about keeping His promise as some people think. He is waiting for you. The Lord does not want any person to be punished forever. He wants all people to be sorry for their sins and turn from them.

2 PETER 3:9

189. PRAISE GOD THAT HE HEARS YOUR PRAYERS!

What if you get distracted while you're praying?

190. YOUR CLASSMATES WHO HAVE LESS THAN YOU

"Give, and it will be given to you. You will have more than enough. It can be pushed down and shaken together and it will still run over as it is given to you. The way you give to others is the way you will receive in return."

LUKE 6:38

191. CHILDREN IN INDIA WHO ARE HUNGRY

Why should we thank God for things that we don't like?

192. YOUR TV WATCHING

I will set no sinful thing in front of my eyes.

PSALM 101:3

193. YOUR SUNDAY SCHOOL TEACHER

Why should we pray even when we don't want to?

194. YOUR SELF-CONTROL

You know that only one person gets a crown
for being in a race even if many people run.
You must run so you will win the crown.

1 CORINTHIANS 9:24

195. PERSECUTED CHRISTIANS LIVING IN LIBYA

Are long prayers better than short ones?

196. IMMIGRANTS IN YOUR COUNTRY

Do not forget to be kind to strangers and let them stay in your home. Some people have had angels in their homes without knowing it.

HEBREWS 13:2

197. YOUR SCHOOL COUNSELOR

Why do some people pray on their knees?

198. PRAISE GOD THAT HE KNOWS YOUR NAME!

"Do not be afraid. For I have bought you and made you free. I have called you by name. You are Mine!"

ISAIAH 43:1

199. YOUR VOLUNTEER PROJECTS

How often should you pray?

200. THANK GOD FOR HIS GRACE!

For by His loving-favor you have been saved from the punishment of sin through faith. It is not by anything you have done. It is a gift of God.

Ephesians 2:8